BALLOON ANIMALS

Jaclyn Crupi

hinkler

About this Book

This book contains everything you need to know to make a range of fun balloon animals.

To make colourful balloon animals, you will need:

- Modelling balloons (lots of them in a range of colours)
- Markers
- Facial-expression stickers
- Googly eyes
- Air pump (you can blow up modelling balloons with your breath but it's very hard and takes a lot of practice!)
- Scissors

Contents

What Are Balloon Animals?

Balloon animals are inflated modelling balloons twisted into shapes to look like animals. The most commonly requested balloon animal is the dog, but it's possible to make a huge range of animals from balloons.

Fun Fact

It takes three times the amount of air pressure to blow up a modelling balloon than it takes to blow up a standard balloon!

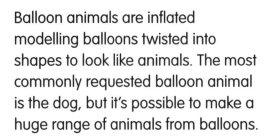

What Are Modelling Balloons?

Modelling balloons are also called twisting balloons. They are long and thin and are perfect for twisting and shaping. Modelling balloons come in a huge range of colours and there are three main sizes, which we'll explain shortly. You cannot use just any long, thin balloon to make balloon animals – they have to be modelling balloons as they're made from thicker plastic and are less likely to break. You can find modelling balloons online or in party, magic or toy stores.

How Do You Make Balloon Animals?

To make balloon animals, you inflate modelling balloons and twist them in specific places to create animal shapes. There are lots of tricks to perfect your balloon animals so they look as cute and colourful as possible, which we'll go through in the next few pages. Some balloon animals are harder to make than others so we'll start simple before we get too twisty!

What Are Balloon Artists?

People who make balloon animals are referred to as balloon artists, balloon twisters or balloon benders! Some people make them for fun while for others it's part of their job to make balloon animals to entertain people.

Which Animals?

In this book you will learn how to make the following balloon animals: dog, snake, swan, giraffe, parrot, elephant, dinosaur, monkey, crocodile, butterfly, mouse, rabbit, octopus and horse. You'll also find instructions for a teddy bear, a sword and a flower. If you follow each twist and turn, you will have a lovely balloon animal menagerie. You'll be popular at parties and your balloon artistry will be in high demand!

Balloon Basics

Before you can start honing your skills as a balloon artist, you need to be comfortable with the main tool of your trade: modelling balloons. These special balloons have some unique properties you should know about.

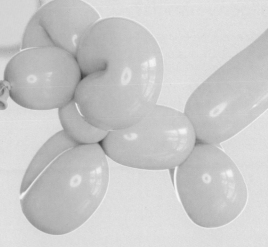

Specific Sizes

Balloon artists mainly use two balloon sizes. The most popular are known as 260s. They're called this because they're approximately 2 inches (5 centimetres) in diameter and 60 inches (152 centimetres) long. The other size most commonly used is 360s. In this book, we will mostly use 260s and will make a note if a different-sized balloon is required.

Almost Pop-proof

Luckily, modelling balloons are made from thick plastic that is designed to be twisted and shaped, so they are less likely to pop than standard balloons. Modelling balloons are thicker than other balloons so they can withstand the pressure of twists. There are a couple of things you can do to reduce the likelihood of a popped balloon:

• Make sure your fingernails are trimmed and don't have any sharp edges. It's easy for a sharp-edged nail to pop a balloon during the animal-making process.
• Don't over-inflate your balloons as this will make them more likely to pop.

Read pages 8 to 9 carefully to learn about how to blow up your balloons.

Multiple Balloons

Some balloon animals use one balloon; some use two or more. Generally, the more balloons twisted into the design the more complicated the balloon animal being constructed. Some balloon artists like to limit the number of balloons they use, but it's good to be able to make both single-balloon and multiple-balloon animals.

Colour Options

Modelling balloons come in a huge range of colours. You certainly won't need to have every colour, but it is good to have a selection. You can choose to make your balloon animals to match the colours of the real animals: for example, you could make a black balloon dog or a brown balloon monkey. Or you can choose to use a bright colour for your balloon animal: for example, you could make an orange balloon crocodile. Metallic modelling balloons are also available and look great.

Top Tip

Many balloon artists like to separate their balloons into size and colour so they can easily find the balloon they want to use. This is especially important when you have a large number of modelling balloons.

Balloon Blowing

The first step to making successful balloon animals is balloon inflation. It's important to blow up each modelling balloon with just the right amount of air. Too much air and it might pop or you could run out of balloon to twist to finish your animal; too little air and it might not stand up.

Inflation and Deflation

There are two ways to blow up your balloons: you can use your breath or you can use an air pump. Modelling balloons are harder to inflate than standard balloons as they are thicker. They require more than three times as much air pressure as a standard balloon takes to blow up, so it's easy to run out of breath and feel lightheaded. If you're serious about making balloon animals, it's worth getting an air pump. It will allow you to pump up multiple balloons quickly and easily. Small, hand-held air pumps are best as you can take them anywhere. Some professional balloon artists use an automatic pump to inflate their balloons.

Breath Inflation

To blow up a balloon, take a big breath and clench your stomach. Place the balloon in your mouth and try not to blow out your cheeks. Use one hand to hold the balloon at your mouth and the other to guide down the balloon as it inflates with your breath. This technique requires a lot of practice. Take it slowly as it's easy to feel lightheaded or out of breath.

Inflation with Air Pump

To blow up a balloon, place the lip of the balloon over the tip of the air pump. Hold the lip of the balloon firmly with one hand so it doesn't come off, then pump backwards and forwards with the other hand. Air will fill the balloon – make sure you keep holding it tightly. If you're having trouble, place the base of the air pump between your knees to hold it in place and this will free both your hands so you can keep one on the balloon and the other can do the pumping.

Burping

No, not burping from your mouth! Balloon burping is when you blow up a balloon as instructed and then release just a little bit of air. This reduces the pressure within the balloon and makes it easier to twist. It's good to get into the habit of using this technique. Burping also makes it less likely that your balloon will pop.

How Much Air?

The amount of air each balloon needs depends on the animal being made and the balloon size being used. We'll tell you in the instructions how much to inflate your balloon for each balloon animal.

How to Tie a Balloon

Tying your balloon keeps the air inside it. Once the balloon is inflated, make sure you have an extra bit of balloon at the lip that you can tie. If you don't, make a twist a little way from the lip of the balloon and release the lip while holding at the twist point. This will give you more space to tie. To tie the balloon, hold the neck (the loose area before the lip of the balloon) between your left thumb and middle finger, with the tip of the balloon pointing up. With your right thumb and index finger, stretch the neck and wrap it around the tips of your left index and middle fingers in a clockwise direction. Spread your left fingers and tuck the balloon end down and through the loop with your right hand. Slide your left fingers out of the loop while holding the tip with your right hand.

Top Tip

Make sure you don't leave your balloons in a hot car or in direct sunlight. They are likely to pop if they get hot.

Twists and Shapes

Balloon animals are formed by twisting inflated modelling balloons into animal shapes. The twisting is simple once you know some key tips and tricks. The most important thing is to always make all your twists in the same direction.

Twisting Motion

If you are right-handed, hold the inflated balloon in your right hand with the tied end pointing towards your left hand. Place your fingers on the top of the balloon and your thumb on the bottom. Push outwards with your thumb and inwards with your fingers to rotate the balloon. Your wrist shouldn't move: just your fingers. This is the motion you will make when creating twists.

Sausage Twist

Using the thumb and pointer finger on your left hand, pinch the balloon near the tied end. When you rotate the balloon with your right hand, you will make your first twist. This is called a sausage twist.

Making Multiple Twists

Hold the twist between the ring finger and little finger of your left hand. This keeps the thumb and pointer finger on your left hand free to pinch the balloon and keep making more twists while your right hand rotates the balloon (always in the same direction). You need to keep holding the first twist between the ring finger and little finger of your left hand and the balloon length in your right hand, or all your twists will come undone.

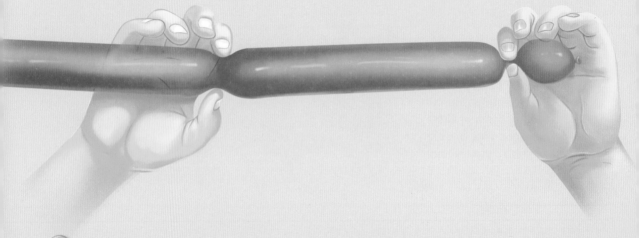

Lock Twist

Lock twists allow you to hold sausage or bubble twists in place. Bubble twists are small sausage twists. Make three sausage twists and bend the balloon so the first twist is parallel with the third twist. Pull the balloon at the bend and twist a few times so the two twists join. They will now stay together, even when you let go of the balloon.

Pinch Twist

Make a small sausage twist (known as a bubble). Fold the balloon so the twists are parallel, pull the sausage/bubble a little and twist it. It will look a little like an ear. There will be times when you need to overtwist pinch twists to prevent air from leaking.

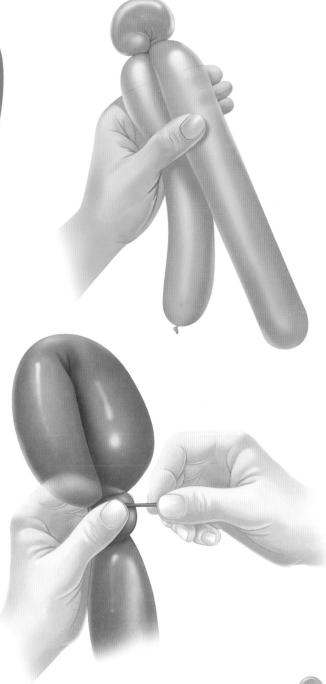

Flower-petal Twist

Flower-petal twists are when you fold a small section of the balloon at the knotted end, twist it while holding the knot and pull the knotted end through the middle of the folded balloon. You can also create flower-petal twists further down the balloon. If a flower-petal twist needs to be done further down the balloon, you can twist the end and lock twist the first and second twists.

Twists and Shapes (continued)

Bend and Squeeze

Bend the balloon, then squeeze it at the bend. Let the air back in and there will still be a bend in the balloon. You can do this multiple times to create bends. Massaging the balloon with your hands while bending it also helps to maintain the bend. The heat from your hands bends the balloon into shape.

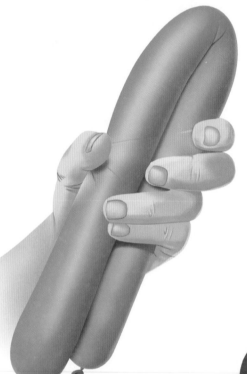

Tulip Twist

Tulip twists involve pushing the tied balloon end inside the balloon. With the index finger on your right hand, push the tied end inside the balloon. Feel for and hold the tied end knot with your left hand on the outside of the balloon. Pull your right index finger out. You may need to squeeze the balloon to make it softer so you can get your finger out. Twist the balloon at the knot and push the knot back in a little bit so that it's resting inside of the balloon.

Poodle Tail

Poodle tails are when you create an air vacuum within the balloon to push air to the balloon tip. To make a poodle tail, you need to squeeze the tip of the balloon and stretch it while pushing the air remaining in the balloon down. This will create a vacuum and push the air to the tip of the balloon. Poodle tails are perfect for dog balloons, obviously, but also when making antennae.

Left-handed?
If you're left-handed, simply reverse these instructions.

Adding Character

There is a lot you can do to add features and details to your balloon animals. You can do this easily with a marker or with facial-expression stickers.

Faces

Drawing a face onto your balloon animal can add some personality and flair. Just take a marker and get to work. You can add a mouth, teeth, nose and eyes if it works with the balloon animal. Remember to add eyelashes and eyebrows for more individuality. Facial-expression stickers also work well.

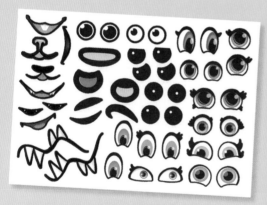

Spots and Stripes

You can add spots, stripes and patches to your balloon tigers, lions and giraffes with markers. This works especially well if you have used the appropriate balloon colour for the animal. Just because you have finished twisting and locking your balloons doesn't mean your animal is finished.

The Balloon Itself

Many balloon animals incorporate the balloon itself into features for the animal. Even a simple dog balloon animal uses the tied knot for the nose and the pointy end for the tail.

Googly Eyes

You can glue googly eyes on to your balloon animals instead of drawing them in with craft glue.

Dog

Sausages and Bubbles
(Unless otherwise stated)
Small bubbles: 1 cm (0.5 inches)
Bubbles: 2.5 cm (1 inch)
Sausages: 6–7 cm (3 inches)

You Will Need:
- One modelling balloon (any colour)
- Balloon pump
- Marker or facial-expression stickers

A dog balloon animal is the perfect place to begin as it uses one of the easier twists. But rather than making just a standard dog shape, we're going to show you how to twist a sausage dog: a dachshund!

How to Twist a Dachshund

1. Inflate the balloon until it's two-thirds full of air. This will leave roughly 15 centimetres (6 inches) un-inflated. Tie a knot.

2. Hold the balloon in your right hand with the tied end pointing towards your left hand.

3. Make three sausage twists of equal length.

4. Make a lock twist by bending the balloon so the first twist is parallel with the third twist. Pull the balloon at the bend and twist so the two twists join. They will now stay together, even when you let go.

5. You have twisted the dog head and ears. Straighten the ears.

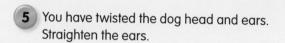

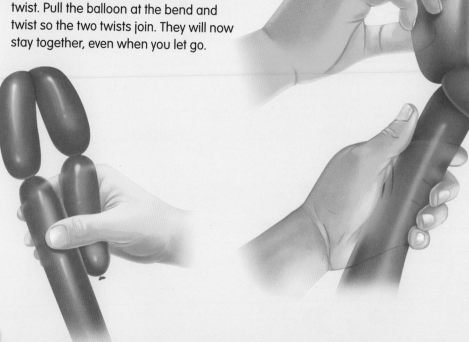

6 Twist a small bubble for the neck and then make two sausage twists.

7 Make a lock twist, just as you did for the dog ears, by bending the balloon so the first sausage twist is parallel with the third twist. Pull the balloon at the bend, then twist so the two twists join. They will now stay together, even when you let go. These are the dog's front legs.

8 As this is a sausage dog, leave a long 10-centimetre (4-inch) section for the body.

9 Make two sausage twists of equal length.

10 Make a lock twist by bending the balloon so the first twist is parallel with the third twist. Pull the balloon at the bend and twist so the two twists join. They will now stay together, even when you let go. These are the dog's rear legs.

11 Straighten it up and your sausage dog is made!

12 Use a marker or stickers to complete the face.

Top Tip

If you wanted to make a poodle instead of a dachshund, follow these instructions and just make the body shorter. To get a poodle tail you need to squeeze the tip of the tail and stretch it while pushing the remaining air in the tail down. This will create a vacuum and push the air to the tip of the tail.

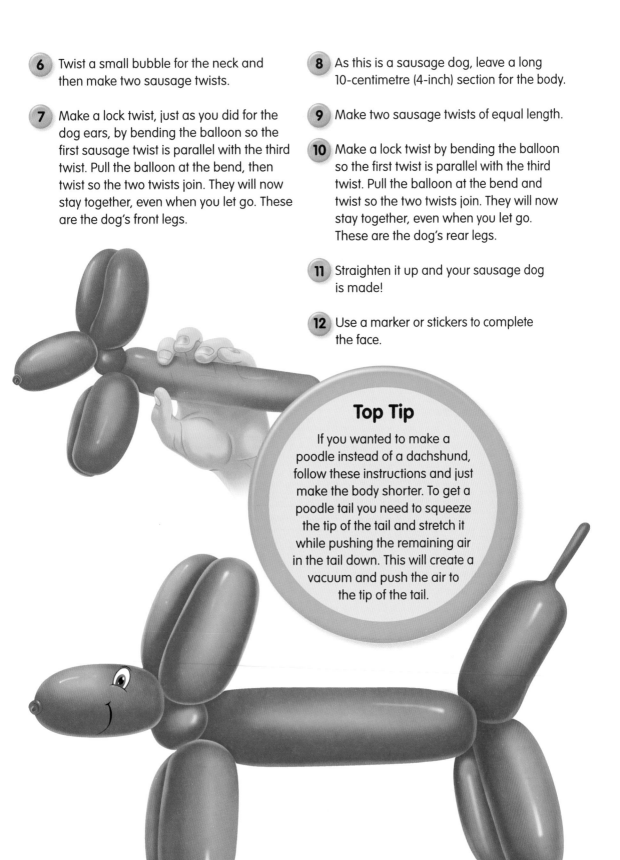

Snake

Sausages and Bubbles
(Unless otherwise stated)
Small bubbles: 1 cm (0.5 inches)
Bubbles: 2.5 cm (1 inch)
Sausages: 6–7 cm (3 inches)

This simple one-balloon animal comes with a twist; it's not just any snake, it's a cobra and you can make it with just one twist!

You Will Need:
• One modelling balloon (any colour)
• Balloon pump
• Marker or facial-expression stickers

How to Twist a Cobra

1. Inflate the balloon all the way and then let all the air out. This will stretch the balloon.

2. Take the deflated balloon and wrap it around two fingers. This will help shape the balloon when you blow it up again.

3. With the balloon still wrapped around your fingers, inflate the balloon again almost all the way. If you are using a hand pump, you will need someone else to pump the balloon for you. Tie a knot.

4. Squeeze the air to the tip of the balloon and twist a small bubble for the head.

5. Fold the balloon and make a medium-sized flower petal. Lock twist it with the twist at the cobra's head.

6. Take the twisted cobra body and feed part of it through the middle of the flower petal. You now have a lying down snake.

7. To make it stand up, bend it over at the neck, pinch it at the bend and release.

8. Use a marker or stickers to complete the face. You can add some scales to the snake body, too.

Swan

This simple one-balloon animal is perfect for beginners who want to get away from all the complicated twists. It's graceful and will even float in your bath!

How to Twist a Swan

1. Inflate the balloon until it's three quarters full of air. This will leave roughly 7 centimetres (3 inches) un-inflated. Tie a knot.

2. Hold the balloon in your right hand with the tied end pointing towards your left hand.

3. Make a sausage twist about 15 centimetres (6 inches) down the balloon.

4. Fold the sausage over the same length and make a flower-petal twist by twisting the balloon while holding the knotted end and then folding the knot through the folded balloon.

5. Make a pinch twist by twisting a small bubble and folding the balloon so the twists are parallel. Pull the bubble a little and twist it.

6. Now go to the long end of the balloon. Fold the tail so it doesn't inflate and roll up the length of balloon, like a snail shell. Massage the balloon gently, as this will make it bend to shape, and release.

7. Twist the swan's head and neck around 180 degrees so that it is facing backwards.

8. Make a twist in the balloon where the swan neck meets the body, leaving it so the head is facing forwards. This twist will rest in the swan body so it shouldn't come undone.

9. Use a marker or stickers to complete the face.

Giraffe

Twisting the long neck of a giraffe is one of the best parts of making this balloon animal! You'll be familiar with the twists for this one, so focus on getting the shape right as that's the most important part.

How to Twist a Giraffe

1 Inflate the balloon nearly all the way, leaving an 8-centimetre (3-inch) tail. Tie a knot.

2 Hold the balloon in your right hand with the tied end pointing towards your left hand.

3 Twist two small bubbles, fold them and lock twist them. Then take the knotted end and wrap it around the centre of the bubbles. This will hold them in place and forms the giraffe's nose.

4 Make a pinch twist by twisting a small bubble and folding the balloon so the twists are parallel. Pull the bubble a little and twist it around the nose twist. You have now made the giraffe's nose and lips.

You Will Need:

- One modelling balloon (any colour)
- Balloon pump
- Marker or facial-expression stickers

Sausages and Bubbles
(Unless otherwise stated)
Small bubbles: 1 cm (0.5 inches)
Bubbles: 2.5 cm (1 inch)
Sausages: 6–7 cm (3 inches)

5 Make a sausage twist for the face.

6 Twist a bubble followed by a small bubble followed by a bubble followed by a small bubble.

7 Make a lock twist by bending the bubble twists so the first twist is parallel with the fifth twist. Pull the balloon at the bend and twist so the two twists join. These will form the horns and ears.

8 Now move to the tip of the balloon. If there is any slack, squeeze the air down the balloon so it fills up the entire balloon.

9 Twist a small bubble for the tail. Twist two sausage twists of the same length and lock twist them by folding the balloon so the tail bubble is parallel with the third twist, then twist them together. These are the hind legs.

10 Make a sausage twist for the giraffe body.

11 Twist two sausage twists of the same length, making sure they are a little longer than the hind legs you twisted in step 9. Lock twist them by folding the balloon so the body sausage twist is parallel with the third twist, then twist them together. These are the front legs.

12 Straighten it up and you have your giraffe.

13 Use a marker or stickers to complete the face. You can also add some spots to the long neck.

Top Tip

Orange and yellow balloons are slightly more prone to bursting, so be sure to massage the balloons after you blow them up if using these colours. This will soften the balloon and make it less likely to burst.

Parrot on a Perch

This is a quick, easy and fun design. It incorporates the parrot as well as a perch for him to sit on.

How to Twist a Parrot on a Perch

1 Inflate the balloon until it's almost full of air. There should be about 2.5 centimetres (1 inch) un-inflated at the end. Tie a knot.

2 Hold the balloon in your right hand with the tied end pointing towards your left hand.

3 Twist a small bubble and then a small sausage. Take the knotted end and twist it around the sausage twist. This will form the parrot's beak and face.

You Will Need:

- One modelling balloon (any colour)
- Balloon pump
- Marker or facial-expression stickers

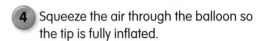

Sausages and Bubbles
(Unless otherwise stated)
Small bubbles: 1 cm (0.5 inches)
Bubbles: 2.5 cm (1 inch)
Sausages: 6–7 cm (3 inches)

4 Squeeze the air through the balloon so the tip is fully inflated.

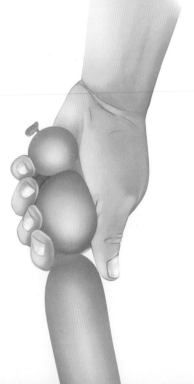

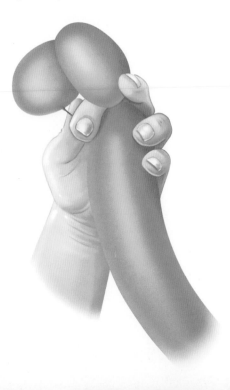

5 At the tip of the balloon, make a large 20-centimetre (8-inch) sausage twist.

6 Lock twist the large sausage twist with the parrot head.

7 Grab the three balloon lengths below the parrot head. 8 centimetres (3 inches) down from the head, twist the three lengths together. This will form the parrot body.

8 Bring the parrot body and head to sit within the large loop. Straighten the parrot so the chest is facing forwards and the head is straight.

9 The parrot is now on its perch with its tail hanging down – a useful handle.

10 Use a marker or stickers to complete the face.

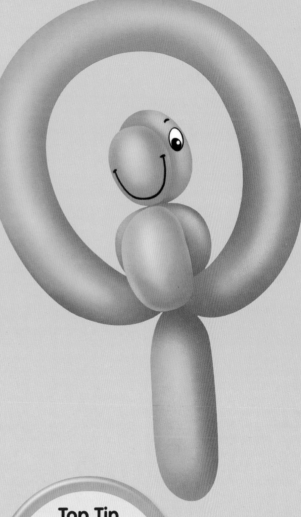

Top Tip

You could tie some string to the top of the loop and hang your Parrot on a Perch outside, in its natural habitat.

Elephant

This elephant may use only one balloon, but there are lots of twists and turns to get that trunk looking just right.

You Will Need:

- One modelling balloon (any colour)
- Balloon pump
- Scissors
- Marker or facial-expression stickers

Sausages and Bubbles
(Unless otherwise stated)
Small bubbles: 1 cm (0.5 inches)
Bubbles: 2.5 cm (1 inch)
Sausages: 6–7 cm (3 inches)

How to Twist an Elephant

1 Inflate the balloon until it's slightly more than half full of air. Tie a knot.

2 Hold the balloon in your right hand with the tied end pointing towards your left hand.

3 To make the trunk shape, fold the end of the balloon into an S-shape and massage it. Release.

4 Make a twist at the end of the trunk bend.

5 Twist a bubble and then twist a sausage. Lock twist the balloon by folding it so the bubble twist and the sausage twist are parallel and twist them together. This is one elephant ear.

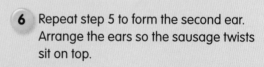

6 Repeat step 5 to form the second ear. Arrange the ears so the sausage twists sit on top.

7 Twist a bubble for the neck and then twist four more bubbles the same size. Lock twist the bubbles by bending the balloon so the first bubble twist is parallel with the fifth twist. Pull the balloon at the bend and twist so the twists join. These are the front legs.

10 You shouldn't have much balloon left at this point but if you do, you need to make a small bubble at the tip and pop it with your fingernail or scissors. Make sure you're still holding the balloon. Slowly let the air out, stopping when you have a small bubble. Pinch twist it so there is a small bubble tail. This is tricky, so go slowly.

11 Use a marker or stickers to complete the face.

Top Tip

This elephant design is especially cute because the head is so large and the body is so small. You could make the body and legs larger if you wish by twisting larger bubbles. If the bend in the trunk is not as pronounced as you'd like, you can massage and bend it once your elephant is complete; just be careful or it could pop.

8 Make a sausage twist to form the body.

9 Twist four bubbles. Lock twist the bubbles by bending the balloon so the first twist is parallel with the fifth twist. Pull the balloon at the bend and twist so the twists join. These are the rear legs.

Dinosaur

A balloon dinosaur is much less scary than the prehistoric version. The dinosaur's spine is super fun to make and involves a new technique where you push twisted bubbles through the body. Unlike the balloon animals so far with the dinosaur we start with the tail and work towards the head.

How to Twist a Dinosaur

Sausages and Bubbles
(Unless otherwise stated)
Small bubbles: 1 cm (0.5 inches)
Bubbles: 2.5 cm (1 inch)
Sausages: 6–7 cm (3 inches)

You Will Need:
• One modelling balloon (any colour)
• Balloon pump
• Marker

1. Inflate the balloon until it's three quarters full of air. This will leave roughly 7 centimetres (3 inches) un-inflated. Tie a knot.

2. Hold the balloon in your right hand with the tied end pointing towards your left hand.

3. Twist three sausage twists, fold the balloon and lock twist the first and third twists together. This is your dinosaur's tail and rear legs.

4. Twist two 12-centimetre (5-inch) sausages, fold the balloon and lock twist them to the legs and tail. This is your dinosaur's body. Ensure you can fit your hand between these two sausages, as this is where you will be pushing the bubbles for the spine.

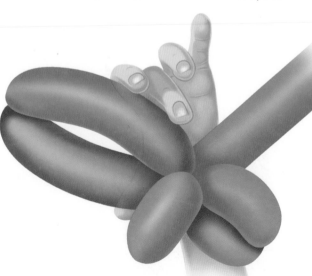

5 Twist five small bubbles.

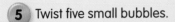

6 Making sure you hold on to the bubbles, push them through the dinosaur's body. This will hold them in place and form the spine.

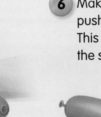

Top Tip

The reason we start with the dinosaur's tail and work towards the head is so the knotted end of the balloon doesn't end up on the face. Unlike many other balloon animals, this wouldn't suit the look of a dinosaur.

7 Twist two sausages, fold the balloon and lock twist them with the dinosaur's body. These are your dinosaur's front legs.

8 The remainder of the balloon will form the dinosaur's neck and head. Bend it gently and massage it to form a neck bend.

9 Take the marker and draw eyes, a nose, a mouth and eyebrows on the dinosaur's face. You can also use the marker to draw scales on the dinosaur's body if you like.

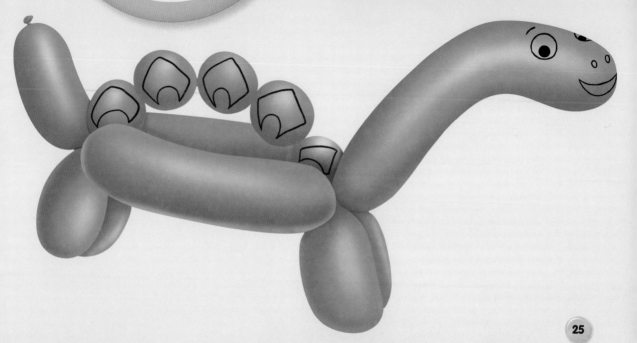

Monkey

Monkeys make perfect balloon animals! The curvy tail is a great feature of this monkey.

How to Twist a Monkey

1 Inflate the balloon until it's about half full of air. Tie a knot.

2 Hold the balloon in your right hand with the tied end pointing toward your left hand.

3 Start by making a flower-petal twist by folding a small section of the balloon at the knotted end. Twist it while holding the knot and pull the knotted end through the middle of the folded balloon.

Sausages and Bubbles
(Unless otherwise stated)
Small bubbles: 1 cm (0.5 inches)
Bubbles: 2.5 cm (1 inch)
Sausages: 6–7 cm (3 inches)

You Will Need:
• One modelling balloon (any colour)
• Balloon pump
• Marker

5 Make a sausage twist and then twist another bubble and make a pinch twist again.

6 Fold the balloon so the two pinch twists are parallel. Pinch twist by holding the two pinch twists out and twist them together. This is tricky, so go slowly. You have now made your monkey head. Position the ears correctly.

4 Make a pinch twist by twisting a small bubble and folding it over, so the twists are parallel. Pull the bubble out a little and twist it.

7 Twist a small bubble for the neck and then twist a sausage followed by two bubbles followed by a sausage for the front legs and paws.

8 Make a lock twist by bending the twists so that the first twist is parallel with the fifth twist. Pull the balloon at the bend and twist so the two twists join.

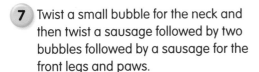

9 Make a sausage twist for the body and then two small sausage twists for the back legs.

10 Fold the balloon so the twists are parallel and lock twist the back legs.

11 At this point, the monkey body is complete but it has a really long tail. To make this look more monkey-like, wrap the tail around your thumb. Squeeze and massage it gently. The tail will now have a nice curve.

12 Take a marker and draw some eyes and facial features on the monkey.

Top Tip

You can easily make this a two-balloon design by adding a tree for your monkey to climb. There is a gap between your monkey's front and back legs. Inflate a green balloon and make a tulip twist at the end. You could add some flower-petal twists if you'd like. Slide the end of the balloon through the gap in the monkey's legs. Slide the monkey up the tree.

Crocodile

Twisting a crocodile is a one-balloon design but it's not as simple as it looks, as many of the twists are small and a little fiddly. Make sure you hold on tightly to your twists as you work through this design.

You Will Need:

- One modelling balloon (any colour)
- Balloon pump
- Marker or facial-expression stickers

Sausages and Bubbles
(Unless otherwise stated)
Small bubbles: 1 cm (0.5 inches)
Bubbles: 2.5 cm (1 inch)
Sausages: 6–7 cm (3 inches)

How to Twist a Crocodile

1 Inflate the balloon until it's a bit over half full of air. Tie a knot.

2 Hold the balloon in your right hand with the tied end pointing towards your left hand.

3 Twist two small bubbles, fold them and lock twist them. Then take the knotted end and wrap it around the centre of the bubbles. This will hold them in place and forms the crocodile's nostrils.

4 Twist another small bubble and pinch twist it.

5 Make a sausage twist. Twist two small bubbles and lock twist them into the sausage twist by folding the balloon and twisting the first twist and the third twist.

6 Squeeze the air to the tip of the balloon. Twist a bubble for the neck and then twist two small sausage twists. Lock twist them into the neck bubble by folding the balloon and twisting the first twist and the third twist.

7 Twist a long sausage twist for the body, then twist two small sausage twists. Lock twist them into the body twist by folding the balloon and twisting the first and the third twists. These are the rear legs.

8 Take the rear legs and pull them apart and then twist them together. This will create two small flower petals.

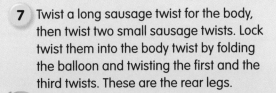

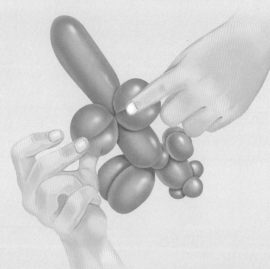

Top Tip

Your balloon animal will look more like a dog than a crocodile for most of the time you're twisting it. Don't worry – it all comes together when you transform the legs with the flower-petal twists!

9 Repeat step 8 with the front legs.

10 Adjust the front legs so they are flat with the body. Adjust the rear legs so they are parallel with the body. The tail and the body should be one straight line.

11 Take the tail and bend it into an S shape. Massage it with your hands and release.

12 Use a marker or stickers to complete the face.

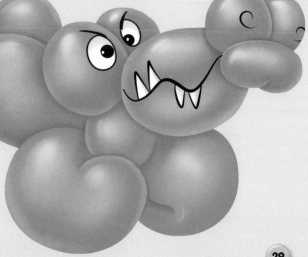

Butterfly

This beautiful two-balloon design looks best when complementary colours are used. The twists joining the two balloons are different to any done before in this book, but they're simple once you get the hang of them.

You Will Need:

• Two modelling balloons (any colours, but it's best to use two complementary colours)
• Balloon pump

Sausages and Bubbles

(Unless otherwise stated)
Small bubbles: 1 cm (0.5 inches)
Bubbles: 2.5 cm (1 inch)
Sausages: 6–7 cm (3 inches)

How to Twist a Butterfly

1 Inflate both balloons until they're three quarters full of air. Tie a knot in each.

2 Hold both balloons in your right hand with the tied ends pointing towards your left hand.

3 Twist two bubbles together at the knotted ends of the balloons.

4 Fold both balloons slightly larger than a sausage to form two small flower petals and lock twist them with the bubbles.

5 Now go to the tip end of the balloons. If necessary, squeeze them so they are even.

6 Twist a sausage twist at the tip of each balloon.

7 Fold the two balloons in half and lock twist the sausage twists at the tip with the flower-petal twists at the end.

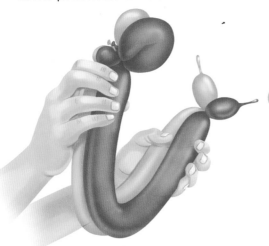

8 Straighten it up so the bubbles are on the bottom and at the back, and so each flower-petal twist matches the colour of the large balloon section it is under. The tip of each balloon should be different to the colour of the large balloon section that it is beneath.

9 Make a poodle tail by squeezing the tip of the balloon and stretching it while pushing down the remaining air in the balloon. This will create a vacuum and push the air to the tip of the balloon. Repeat this with the other balloon tip.

Top Tip

You can easily use elastic or ribbon to attach these butterfly wings to your shoulders so you can wear them. Just thread some elastic or ribbon loops through each large wing section and place them over your shoulders.

10 Shape the wings by pulling them and massaging them a little until you're happy with their shape.

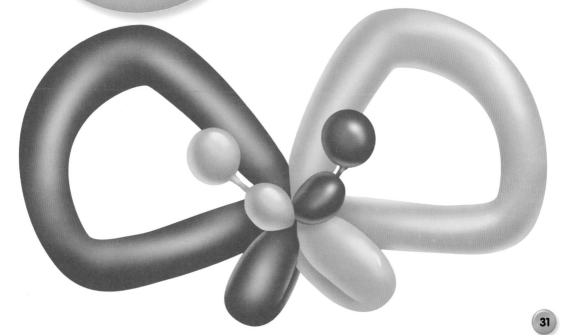

Mouse

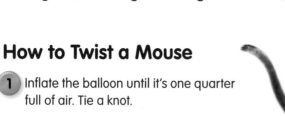

A balloon-animal mouse is much cuter and less trouble than the real thing! This is a fairly simple design but looks great, so let's get twisting!

You Will Need:

• One modelling balloon (any colour)
• Balloon pump
• Marker or facial-expression stickers

Sausages and Bubbles
(Unless otherwise stated)
Small bubbles: 1 cm (0.5 inches)
Bubbles: 2.5 cm (1 inch)
Sausages: 6–7 cm (3 inches)

How to Twist a Mouse

1. Inflate the balloon until it's one quarter full of air. Tie a knot.

2. Hold the balloon in your right hand with the tied end pointing towards your left hand.

3. Twist a bubble, then twist a flower petal by folding the balloon and twisting at the bubble twist.

4. Twist another flower petal the same size as the first one. These are the ears.

5 Twist a small bubble for the neck, then twist two small bubbles for the front legs. Lock twist the legs by folding the balloon and twisting the first twist and the third twist together.

6 Twist a small bubble for the body, then twist two bubbles the same size for the rear legs. Lock twist the legs by folding the balloon and twisting the first twist and the third twist together.

7 Twist a tiny bubble in the remaining end of the balloon. Pull it and pinch twist it. The remaining un-inflated balloon is the tail.

8 Adjust the mouse so the ears and body are straight.

9 Hold the knot on the mouse's head and then pull it and wrap it back around the ears. Leave the knot there.

10 Take a marker and draw a nose, whiskers, a mouth and eyes. You could also use facial-expression stickers.

Top Tip

You will need to manage the air in the balloon for this design to ensure you have enough air to twist the rear legs and create the small tail. Be sure to check how much air you have left as you work through, and squeeze some air down the balloon if needed.

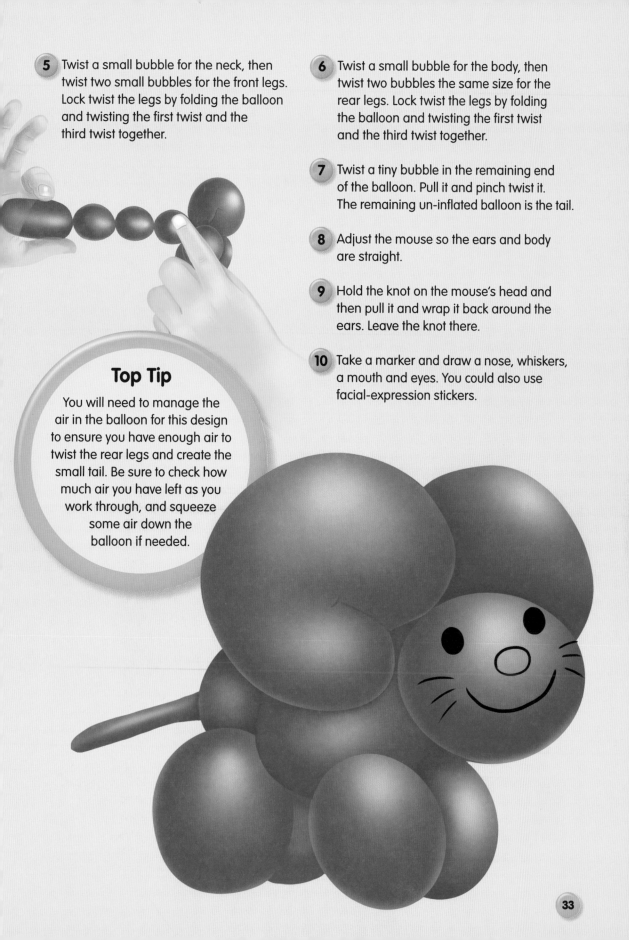

Rabbit

It's time to twist an adorable little bunny rabbit! This balloon animal uses two balloons: one for the body and one for the eyes. This is a challenging design, so hold onto your twists and go slowly.

You Will Need:

- Two modelling balloons (any colours)
- Balloon pump
- Scissors
- Marker

Sausages and Bubbles
(Unless otherwise stated)
Small bubbles: 1 cm (0.5 inches)
Bubbles: 2.5 cm (1 inch)
Sausages: 6–7 cm (3 inches)

How to Twist a Rabbit

1. Take the balloon you will be using for the eyes and cut it so it's roughly 5 centimetres (2 inches) long. Keep the rest of the balloon, as you can use it to make more eyes (see top tip on page 36). Inflate it about 4 centimetres (1.5 inches) and tie a knot.

2. Twist the eye balloon in the middle. Tie the ends together in a knot. Set aside.

3. Inflate the body balloon until it's three quarters full of air. This will leave roughly 7 centimetres (3 inches) un-inflated. Tie a knot.

4. Hold the balloon in your right hand with the tied end pointing towards your left hand.

5. Twist a bubble and wrap the knotted end of the balloon around the twist in a pinch twist. This is the rabbit's tail.

6. Twist a sausage twist and two bubbles, then lock twist the bubbles together. These are the rabbit's cheeks.

7 Take the eyes you made and place them over the two cheek bubbles you just twisted. You will need to hold the eyes in place while doing the next step.

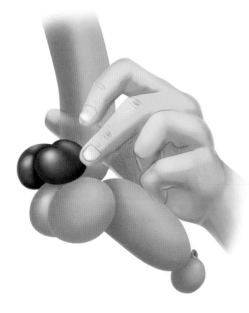

8 Wrap the balloon length over the eyes and cheeks. Twist the balloon length at the point where it meets the cheeks and lock twist the balloon length into the neck. This will require you to stretch the balloon a little, but don't worry: it shouldn't pop. You now have the rabbit's head.

9 Twist two sausages and lock twist them to the pinch-twisted tail.

10 Twist two more sausages and lock twist them to the rabbit's neck.

11 Twist a bubble at the end of the remaining balloon.
(Continued over)

Rabbit (continued)

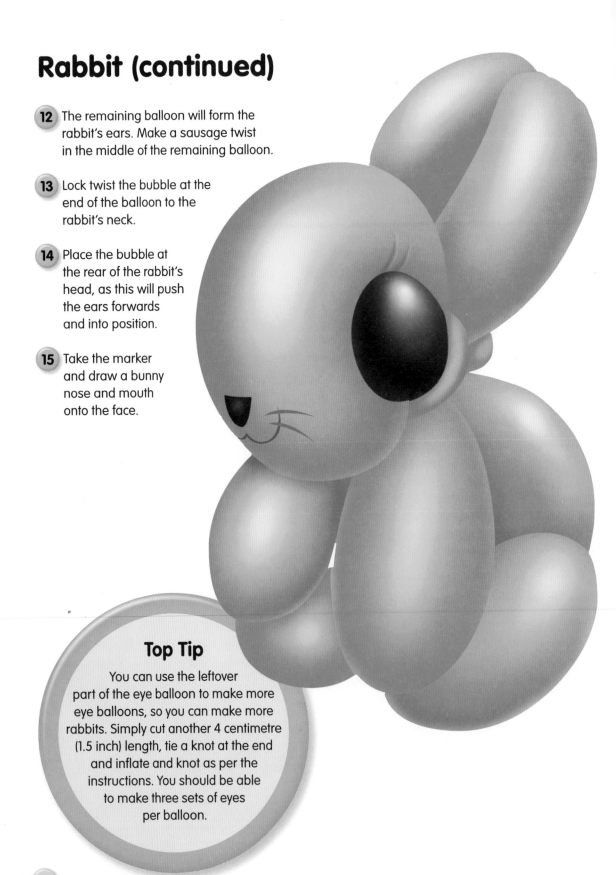

12 The remaining balloon will form the rabbit's ears. Make a sausage twist in the middle of the remaining balloon.

13 Lock twist the bubble at the end of the balloon to the rabbit's neck.

14 Place the bubble at the rear of the rabbit's head, as this will push the ears forwards and into position.

15 Take the marker and draw a bunny nose and mouth onto the face.

Top Tip

You can use the leftover part of the eye balloon to make more eye balloons, so you can make more rabbits. Simply cut another 4 centimetre (1.5 inch) length, tie a knot at the end and inflate and knot as per the instructions. You should be able to make three sets of eyes per balloon.

Octopus

Even eight-legged animals can be twisted into balloon shapes! This three-balloon animal will have you making some serious twists, but it's a very fun balloon animal.

You Will Need:

- Two modelling balloons (any colour but it's best to use the same colour for both balloons)
- One 13-centimetre (5-inch) white round balloon
- Balloon pump • Scissors
- Marker or facial-expression stickers

Sausages and Bubbles
(Unless otherwise stated)
Small bubbles: 1 cm (0.5 inches)
Bubbles: 2.5 cm (1 inch)
Sausages: 6–7 cm (3 inches)

How to Twist an Octopus

1. Inflate the first balloon until it's half full of air. Tie a knot.

2. Hold the balloon in your right hand with the tied end pointing towards your left hand.

3. Push the air down the balloon and massage it to try to make it soft.

4. To make the first tentacle, fold the end of the balloon into an S shape and massage it. Release.

5. Make a twist at the end of the tentacle bend.

6. Make two sausage twists and lock twist them together.

7. Wrap the balloon length over the lock twisted sausage twists. Twist the end of the balloon length at the point it meets the lock twist. Lock twist these two twists together.

(Continued over)

Octopus (continued)

8 To make another tentacle, fold the remaining end of the balloon into an S shape and massage it. Release.

9 If you have any balloon remaining, tie the end and cut it.

10 Now take your second balloon and inflate it until it's half full of air. Tie a knot.

11 Push the air down the balloon and massage it to make it soft.

12 To make the first tentacle, fold the end of the balloon into an S-shape and massage it. Release.

13 Make a twist at the end of the tentacle bend.

14 Fold the balloon and make a small flower petal. Twist the end and lock twist it with the twist at the tentacle bend.

15 Make three more flower petals and lock twist each one.

16 To make another tentacle, fold the remaining end of the balloon into an S shape and massage it. Release.

17 Bring the two balloons together, locating the sections where the tentacles meet, and lock twist them together. You will have four long tentacles and four folded tentacles.

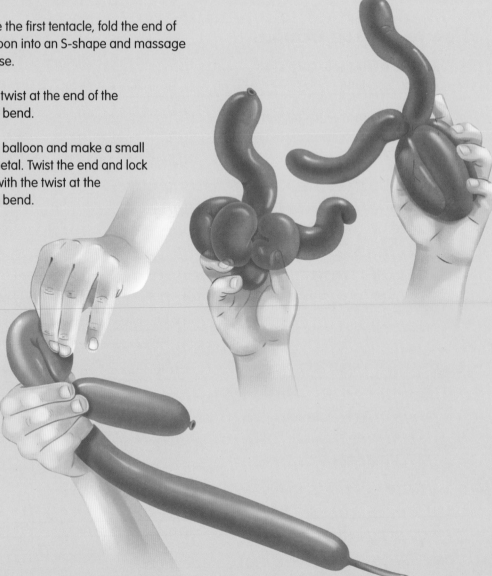

18 Take one of the long tentacles and move it in between one of the folded tentacles. Do this to all the tentacles, alternating a long tentacle with a folded tentacle.

19 Inflate a white 13-centimetre (5-inch) balloon to the size of a small lemon. Tie a knot. Twist the balloon in half and wrap the knotted end around the centre of the twist once or twice to hold it in place.

20 Thread the white eyes balloon into the octopus head so one eye sits on either side of the nose.

21 Use a marker or stickers to complete the face.

Top Tip

Carefully insert a straw or other non-pointed stick into the base of the octopus. This will allow you to hold the octopus without touching it, so you can make it move as it would in the water.

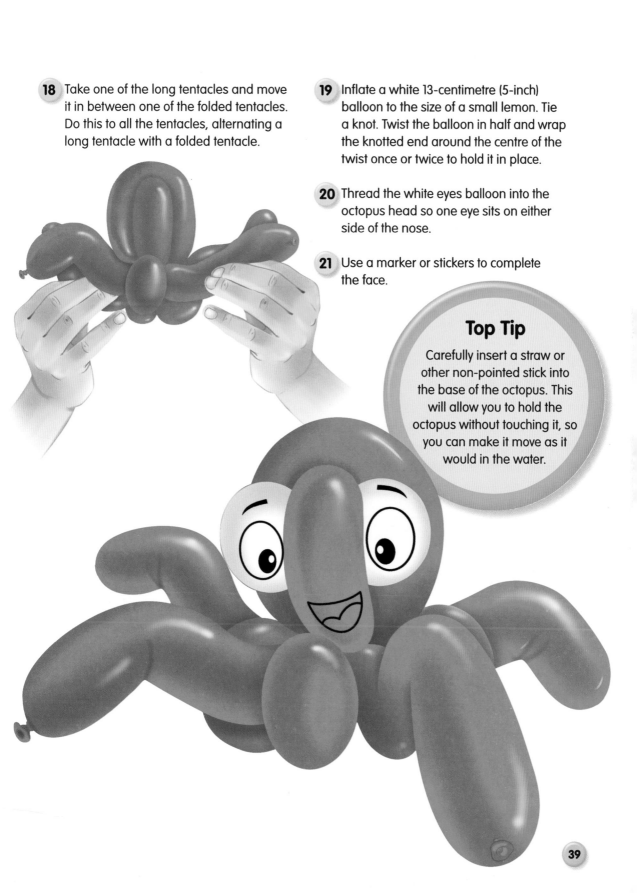

Horse

This is a two-balloon animal. You need to be fairly confident to make this one, but the result is super cool so do your best!

Sausages and Bubbles
(Unless otherwise stated)
Small bubbles: 1 cm (0.5 inches)
Bubbles: 2.5 cm (1 inch)
Sausages: 6–7 cm (3 inches)

You Will Need:
• Two modelling balloons (any colour, but it's best to use two different colours)
• Balloon pump
• Scissors
• Marker

How to Twist a Horse

1. Inflate the body balloon until it's three quarters full of air. This will leave roughly 7 centimetres (3 inches) un-inflated. Tie a knot.

2. Hold the balloon in your right hand with the tied end pointing towards your left hand.

3. Twist two very small bubbles and twist them together. Take the slack of the knot and wrap it around the middle of the bubbles. These are the nostrils.

4. Make a pinch twist by twisting a small bubble and folding it over, so the twists are parallel. Pull the bubble out a little and twist it.

5. Make a sausage twist and then twist two bubbles. Lock twist the bubbles by bending the balloon so the first twist is parallel with the second twist. Pull the balloon at the bend and twist so the two twists join.

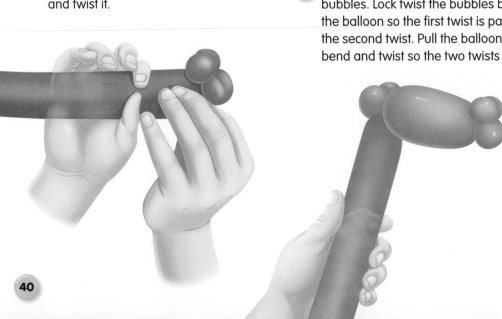

6 Make a sausage twist for the neck. Horses have long necks, so make the sausage twist about 10 centimetres (4 inches) long.

7 Make two sausage twists for the horse's front legs and lock twist them by bending the balloon, so the first twist is parallel with the third twist. Pull the balloon at the bend and twist so the two twists join. These are the horse's front legs.

8 Make a small sausage twist for the horse's body.

9 Make two sausage twists for the horse's rear legs and lock twist them by bending the balloon so the first twist is parallel with the third twist. Pull the balloon at the bend and twist so the two twists join.

10 Pinch twist the small tail at the base of the horse. The horse's body is now complete.

11 Inflate the mane balloon until it's about a third full of air. Tie a knot.

12 Take the knotted end of the mane balloon and wrap it where the neck and the front legs of the horse meet.

13 Twist four bubbles on the mane balloon and lock twist the final twist to where the ears meet on the body balloon.

14 Twist another four bubbles on the mane balloon and lock twist the final twist to where the neck and the front legs of the horse meet.
(Continued over)

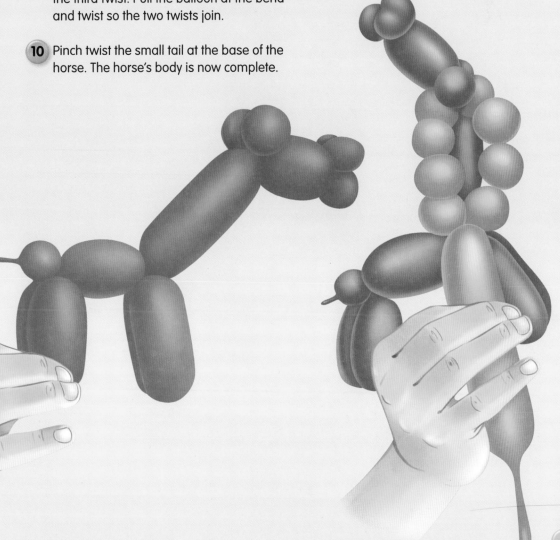

Horse (continued)

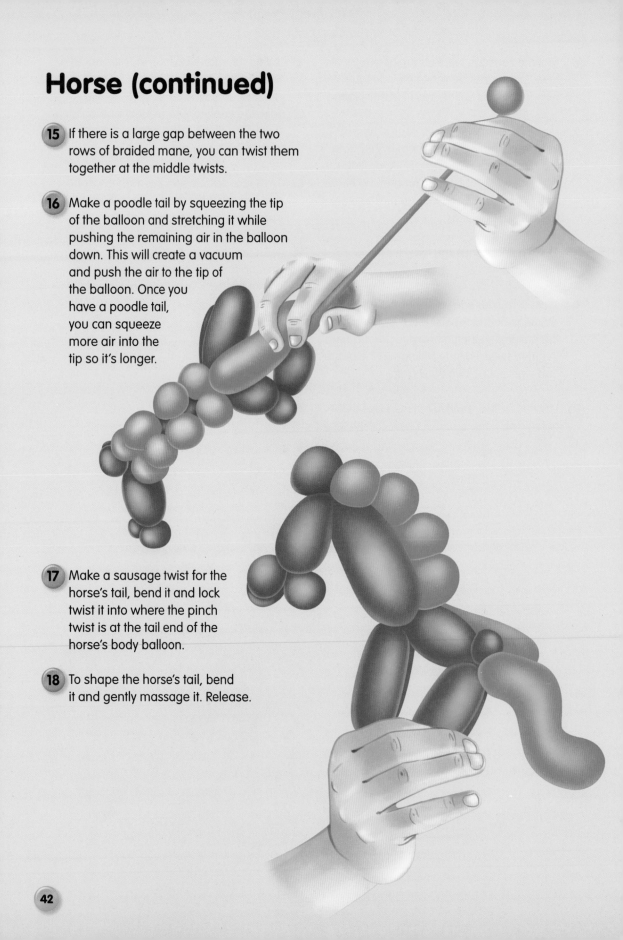

15 If there is a large gap between the two rows of braided mane, you can twist them together at the middle twists.

16 Make a poodle tail by squeezing the tip of the balloon and stretching it while pushing the remaining air in the balloon down. This will create a vacuum and push the air to the tip of the balloon. Once you have a poodle tail, you can squeeze more air into the tip so it's longer.

17 Make a sausage twist for the horse's tail, bend it and lock twist it into where the pinch twist is at the tail end of the horse's body balloon.

18 To shape the horse's tail, bend it and gently massage it. Release.

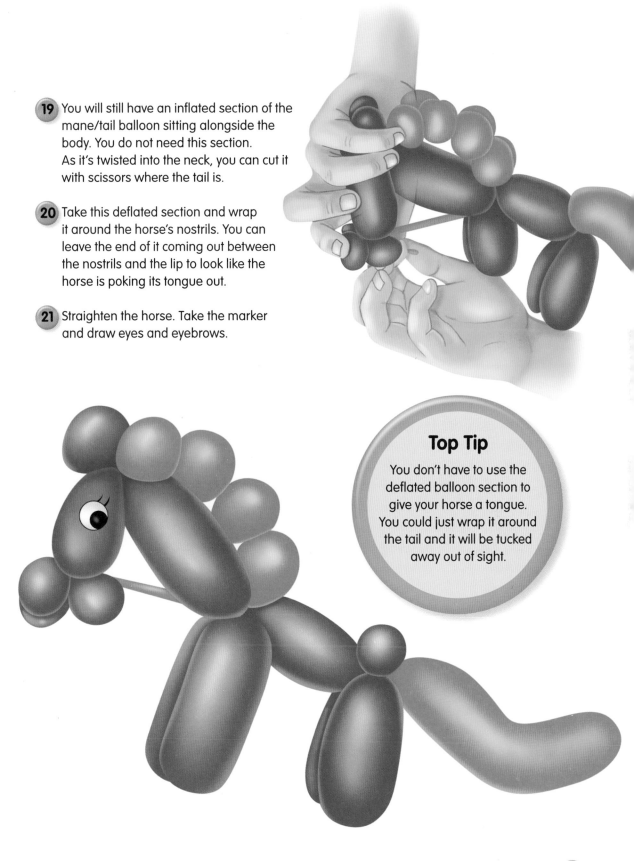

19 You will still have an inflated section of the mane/tail balloon sitting alongside the body. You do not need this section. As it's twisted into the neck, you can cut it with scissors where the tail is.

20 Take this deflated section and wrap it around the horse's nostrils. You can leave the end of it coming out between the nostrils and the lip to look like the horse is poking its tongue out.

21 Straighten the horse. Take the marker and draw eyes and eyebrows.

Top Tip

You don't have to use the deflated balloon section to give your horse a tongue. You could just wrap it around the tail and it will be tucked away out of sight.

Sword & Flower

You can make other objects besides animals with modelling balloons. In fact, there are loads of objects you can make. Here we'll show you how to make a simple balloon flower and a balloon sword.

Sausages and Bubbles
(Unless otherwise stated)
Small bubbles: 1 cm (0.5 inches)
Bubbles: 2.5 cm (1 inch)
Sausages: 6–7 cm (3 inches)

You Will Need:
• One modelling balloon (any colour)
• Balloon pump

How to Twist a Sword

1 Inflate the balloon until it's almost full of air. There should be about 2.5 centimetres (1 inch) un-inflated at the end. Tie a knot.

2 Hold the balloon in your right hand with the tied end pointing towards your left hand.

3 Take the balloon and fold it twice. This will give you three balloon sections.

4 Grab the three balloon sections in the middle of the fold and twist them together.

5 Straighten the two loops and handle.

How to Twist a Flower

1. Inflate the stem balloon until it's almost full of air. Let out a little air and tie a knot.

2. Fold the balloon into three equal sections. Twist all three sections in the middle.

Sausages and Bubbles
(Unless otherwise stated)
Small bubbles: 1 cm (0.5 inches)
Bubbles: 2.5 cm (1 inch)
Sausages: 6–7 cm (3 inches)

You Will Need:
- Two modelling balloons (any colours)
- Balloon pump

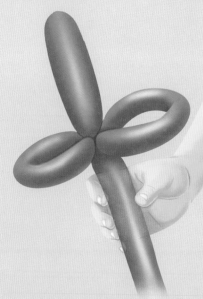

5. Make as many flower-petal twists of the same size as you can with the air in your balloon.

3. Inflate the flower balloon until it's a bit over half full of air. Tie a knot.

4. Make a flower-petal twist and use the knotted end to go through the centre of the flower petal to keep it in place.

6. Wrap the tip of the balloon around the flower-petal twists.

7. Take the stem balloon and twist a bubble at the tip. Feed the bubble into the middle of the flower-petal twists.

Top Tip

You can shape the leaves of the flower stem by massaging them. You can also bend the top of the stem forwards by bending and massaging it. That way your flower faces forwards rather than upwards.

Teddy Bear

The pinch twists in this design are tricky and can easily pop the balloon. If this happens, don't worry as it does take practice to perfect pinch twists.

You Will Need:

- One modelling balloon (any colour)
- Balloon pump
- Marker or facial-expression stickers

Sausages and Bubbles

(Unless otherwise stated)
Small bubbles: 1 cm (0.5 inches)
Bubbles: 2.5 cm (1 inch)
Sausages: 6–7 cm (3 inches)

How to Twist a Teddy Bear

1 Inflate the balloon until it's slightly more than half full of air. Tie a knot.

2 Hold the balloon in your right hand with the tied end pointing towards your left hand.

3 Twist a bubble then twist two small bubbles. Now twist five bubbles. Over-twist all these bubbles, as they can leak air.

4 Lock twist the balloon by bending it so the first bubble (the one after the two small bubbles) and the fifth bubble are parallel, then lock twist them together.

5 The five bubbles form a loop. Take the first bubble you twisted and push it through this loop, leaving the two small bubbles. These will sit behind the head.

6 Pinch twist the ears by taking the bubble on either side of the head, pulling it gently and twisting it.

7 Twist a small bubble for the neck and then twist another small bubble. Fold the balloon over and pinch twist the second bubble.

8 Twist a sausage, a small bubble, another small bubble then another sausage.

9 Lock twist the arms by folding the balloon and lock twisting the first sausage twist with the last sausage twist.

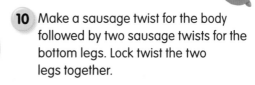

10 Make a sausage twist for the body followed by two sausage twists for the bottom legs. Lock twist the two legs together.

11 Use a marker or stickers to complete the face.

Top Tip

It's important to over twist the five bubbles in step three. This is because air can leak from the ears and cheeks if you don't. By over twisting these bubbles, you ensure that the shape of your teddy bear's face stays nice and rounded in all sections.

Clowning Around

There is a theatre to making balloon animals. Once you've mastered twisting the animals in this book, try adding some drama, humour and fun to your balloon twisting by inviting an audience to watch you create all the cute animals from this book.

Speed

One of the main ways you can impress your audience is by twisting your balloons quickly. The crowd won't be able to tell what you're making, so they'll be super impressed when they see the cool finished result!

Outfit

Dress to impress. Many clowns create balloon animals, but you don't have to dress as a clown. You're a balloon-animal-making entertainer though, so dress the part and wow your audience. Bright colours always work well!

Jokes

Feel free to tell animal jokes as you twist your balloons. Everybody loves a good joke and they're sure to make your friends smile!

Animal Choices

Help your audience members choose the balloon animals they would like by offering a choice of all the balloon animals you can make. You don't want people requesting animals you don't know how to make yet!

Hands

It's hard to make balloon animals while wearing gloves or with sweaty hands. You can dust your hands with talcum powder if they're sweaty and just don't wear gloves!